I WONDER Why

Pyramids Were Built

and other questions
about ancient Egypt

Philip Steele

KINGFISHER
NEW YORK

KINGFISHER
LONDON & NEW YORK

Copyright © 2011 by Kingfisher
Published in the United States by Kingfisher,
175 Fifth Ave., New York, NY 10010
Kingfisher is an imprint of Macmillan Children's Books, London.
All rights reserved.

First published in 1995 by Kingfisher
This edition published 2011 by Kingfisher

Distributed in the U.S. by Macmillan, 175 Fifth Ave.,
New York, NY 10010
Distributed in Canada by H.B. Fenn and Company Ltd.,
34 Nixon Road, Bolton, Ontario L7E 1W2

LIBRARY OF CONGRESS CATALOGING-IN-PUBLICATION DATA
has been applied for.

ISBN 978-0-7534-6558-5 (HC)
ISBN 978-0-7534-6527-1 (PB)

Kingfisher books are available for special promotions and
premiums. For details contact: Special Markets Department,
Macmillan, 175 Fifth Ave., New York, NY 10010.

For more information, please visit www.kingfisherbooks.com

Printed in China
9 8 7 6 5 4 3 2 1
1TR/1010/WKT/UTD/140MA

Consultant: Department of Egyptian Antiquities, British Museum
Illustrations: Simone Boni (Virgil Pomfret Agency) 16–17; Peter
Dennis (Linda Rogers Associates) 14–15, 24–25, 28–29; Chris
Forsey cover, 12–13; Luigi Galante (Virgil Pomfret Agency)
4–5; Nick Harris (Virgil Pomfret Agency) 18–19, 22–23; Adam
Hook (Linden Artists) 8–9, 26–27, 30–31; Tony Kenyon (B.L.
Kearley) all cartoons; Nicki Palin 6–7, 10–11, 20–21.

CONTENTS

Why do we call Egyptians ancient?

We call the Egyptians ancient because they lived such a long time ago—not because they all reached a ripe old age! The first Egyptians were farmers about 8,000 years ago. Within a few thousand years, Egypt had become one of the most powerful countries in the world.

Will people be studying us in 5,000 years? What will they think about the way we live now?

The Egyptians usually built tombs for dead kings on the river's western bank, where the Sun sets. They believed that their kings went to meet the Sun god when they died.

Egypt is mostly sandy desert, where nothing grows. The ancient Egyptians settled on the banks of the Nile River, where there was plenty of water for themselves and their crops.

Why were the Egyptians great?

The Egyptians were so good at farming that they became very rich. They built fantastic temples for their gods and huge pointed tombs called pyramids where they buried their kings. They had armies and ships and courts of law. Their priests studied the stars, and their craftspeople made beautiful things from gold and silver.

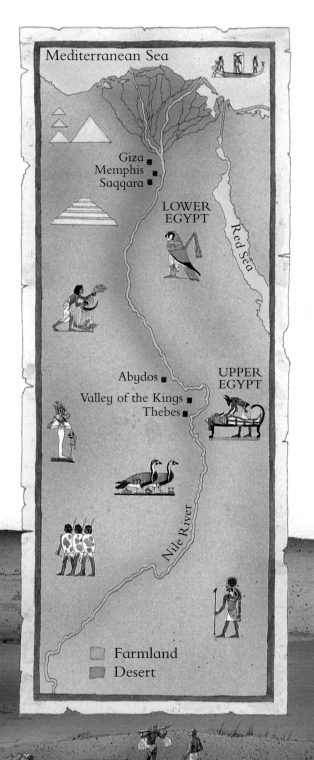

Mediterranean Sea

Giza
Memphis
Saqqara

LOWER EGYPT

Red Sea

Abydos
Valley of the Kings
Thebes

UPPER EGYPT

Nile River

Farmland
Desert

Who ruled Egypt?

The king of Egypt was called the pharaoh. The Egyptians believed that their Sun god, Re, was the first king of Egypt and that all the pharaohs after him were his relatives. This made the pharaoh very holy—and very powerful! The people thought he was a god on Earth.

The pharaoh's advisers were called the Honored Ones. There were all kinds of royal officials, too, with fancy names like the Director of Royal Dress and the Keeper of the Royal Wigs.

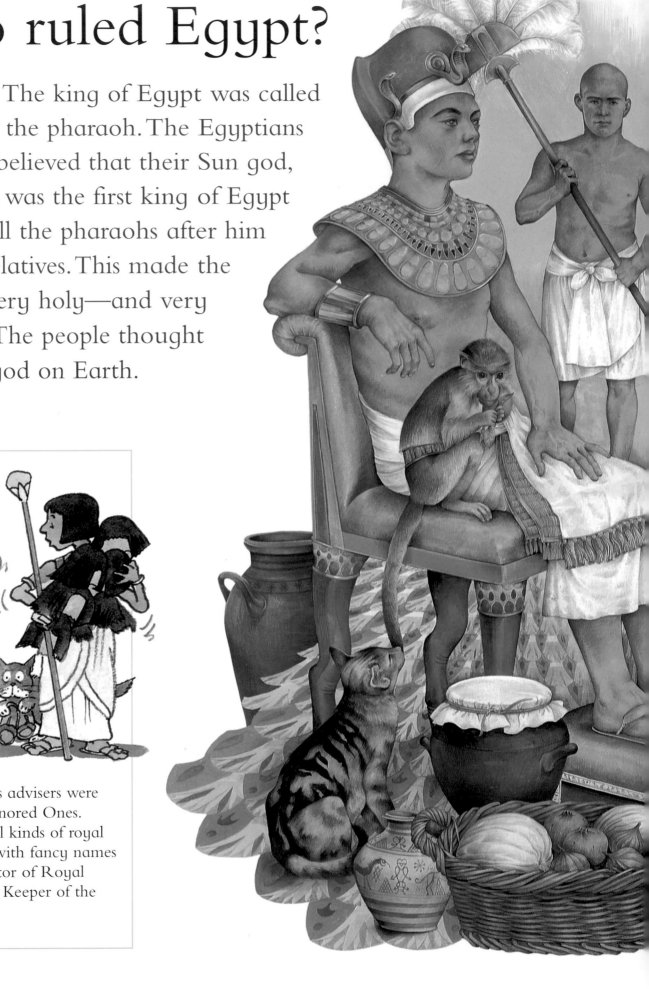

Could a woman be pharaoh?

Although very few women ruled Egypt, there was a famous female pharaoh named Hatshepsut. When her six-year-old nephew came to the throne, Hatshepsut was asked to rule Egypt for him—just until he was a little older. But Hatshepsut liked ruling so much that she wouldn't let her nephew take over. He didn't get the chance to rule until he was 30 years old!

When she was pharaoh, Hatshepsut had to wear the badges of royalty. These included a false beard made of real hair.

How would you know if you met a pharaoh?

He would be wearing a crown, of course! In fact, pharaohs sometimes wore two crowns at the same time—a white one for Upper Egypt, which was the southern part of the country, and a red one for Lower Egypt, which was in the north.

Who was the crocodile god?

In old paintings and carvings, most Egyptian gods and goddesses have animal heads. The water god, Sebek, was shown as a crocodile. Thoth had the head of a bird called an ibis, while Taweret looked like a hippopotamus! Osiris and Isis were luckier. They were shown as a great king and queen.

The Egyptians loved to wear lucky charms. Their favorites were scarabs. The scarab beetle was sacred to the sun god, Re.

The ancient Egyptians worshiped as many as 2,000 gods and goddesses!

Thoth, god of learning

Osiris, god of death

Who was the goddess Nut?

Nut was the goddess of the heavens, and she was usually shown covered in stars. Many gods and goddesses were linked in families. Nut was married to Geb, and Isis and Osiris were their children.

Being a priest was a part-time job. Most priests spent only three months a year at the temple and lived at home the rest of the time.

Taweret, goddess of childbirth and babies

Isis, wife of Osiris

Priests had to wash twice during the day and twice at night to make themselves clean and pure for the gods.

Why did the Egyptians bury their mummies?

A mummy is a dead body that has been dried out so it lasts for thousands of years. The Egyptians believed that the dead traveled to another world, where they needed their bodies. And they didn't want any parts to be missing!

Some poorer families had their nearest and dearest mummified, but it was an expensive business. Only the rich could afford a really good sendoff.

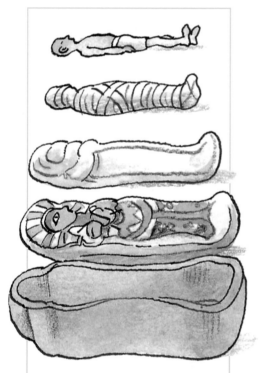

The mummy was placed inside a series of wooden coffins. The coffins were then put in a big stone case called a sarcophagus.

Monkeys, crocodiles, cats, and other sacred animals were often mummified, too!

Why were mummies brainless?

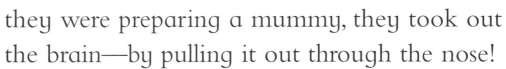

The ancient Egyptians believed that the heart was the most important part of the whole body. They thought that the brain was useless. So when they were preparing a mummy, they took out the brain—by pulling it out through the nose!

Why were mummies wrapped in bandages?

Wrapping the dead body helped keep its shape. After the insides were removed, the body was dried out for 40 days in salty stuff called natron. Then it was washed, rubbed with ointments, and tightly bandaged.

Why were the pyramids built?

The Great Pyramid of Giza was built more than 4,500 years ago. This is what it looks like today.

The pyramids were huge tombs for dead pharaohs and other very important people. No one knows exactly why the pyramids were shaped the way they were. Some people think they were built to point toward the Sun and stars so that the dead person's spirit could fly to heaven like a rocket.

Pharaohs were buried with all their finest clothes and jewelry, so tombs were given sneaky traps to catch robbers.

There are other, smaller pyramids at Giza—and more than 80 at other places in Egypt. Some have stepped sides and bent tops.

This is what the
Great Pyramid
looks like
inside.

Pharaoh's
chamber

Who liked to get knee-deep in mud?

Egyptian farmers loved mud—it has all the water and nutrients that plants need in order to grow well. The most important time in a farmer's year was when the Nile River flooded and dumped rich, black mud onto the dry fields. A good flood meant a good harvest. A bad one meant people went hungry.

Priests watched the Moon and stars to figure out a calendar of the months. This told them when the floods would come and when to plant crops.

Juicy grapes and fresh green vegetables were grown in the rich Nile mud. Golden ears of wheat and barley were harvested and stored in granaries.

The only farmland in Egypt is near the Nile River. It used to be called the Black Land because the mud left by the floods was black. The rocky desert was called the Red Land.

Which was the fastest way to travel?

The quickest route in Egypt was the Nile River. Egyptian boats were made from river reeds or wood. They were the only way to get from one side of the river to the other—unless you swam and liked crocodiles!

The big question each year was "How deep is the flood?" Notched stones were used like giant rulers to measure the rising water. The stones were called nilometers.

Farmers dug ditches to carry water to their crops when the Nile wasn't in flood. They used a clever machine called a shadoof to lift water out of the river into the ditches.

Why did people sit on the roof?

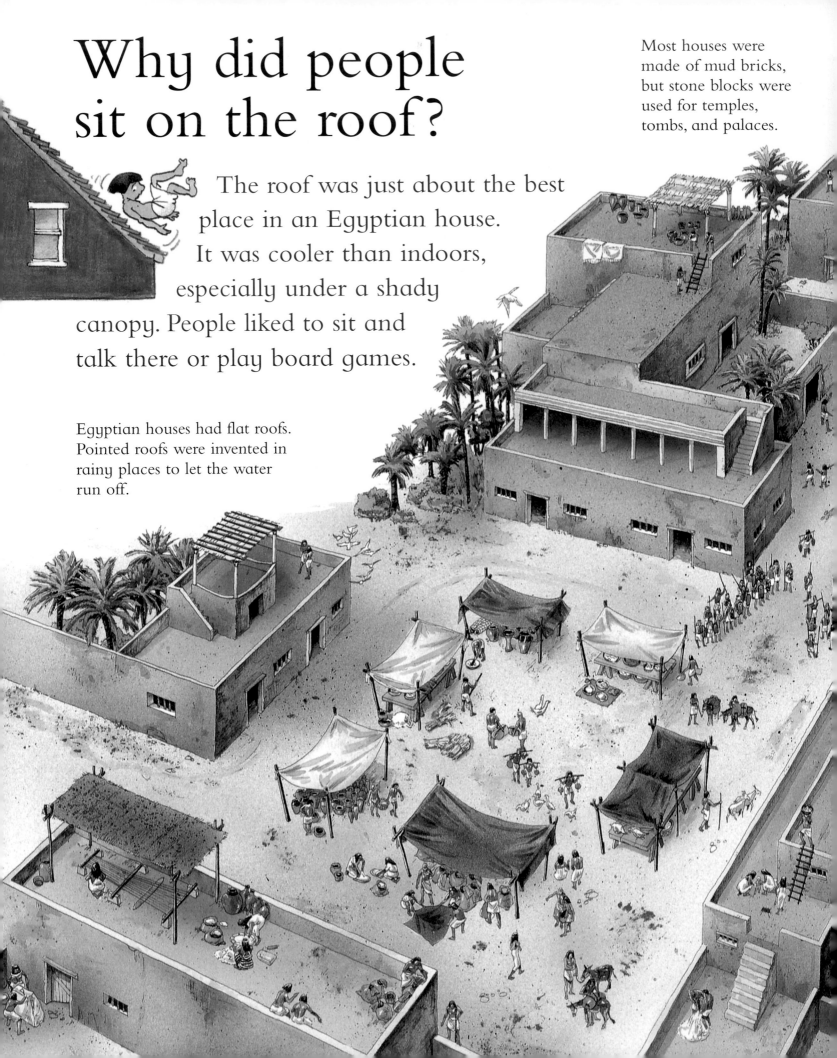

The roof was just about the best place in an Egyptian house. It was cooler than indoors, especially under a shady canopy. People liked to sit and talk there or play board games.

Most houses were made of mud bricks, but stone blocks were used for temples, tombs, and palaces.

Egyptian houses had flat roofs. Pointed roofs were invented in rainy places to let the water run off.

Who made mud pies?

Bricks were made from river mud. Brickmakers trampled the mud with their bare feet until it was sticky. They added pieces of straw and reed to make the mixture firmer. Then they shaped the mud pies into bricks, which dried hard in the sun.

Who had nightmares?

Some Egyptians must have slept well, but their beds look very uncomfortable! They were made of wood, with ropes or leather straps instead of springs. And people didn't lie on soft pillows filled with feathers. All they had were wooden headrests!

Who had floury feet?

When Egyptian cooks made bread, they sometimes jumped into a huge bowl on the floor and kneaded the dough with their feet. Let's hope they washed them first!

Egyptian feet were good at making wine, too. Every last drop of juice was trampled from the grapes.

The Egyptians baked a lot of delicious cakes—doughnuts, pyramid-shaped buns, and cakes that looked like crocodiles!

What's the world's stalest bread?

Loaves of bread have been found in Egyptian tombs. No one has tasted them, though. The bread is thousands of years old and as hard as a rock!

Wooden lunch boxes full of meat and fruit were sometimes left in tombs in case the mummy got hungry in the next world!

Egyptian bread must have been a bit gritty, even when it was fresh, since many of the mummies' teeth are very worn down.

Who had splendid feasts?

Well, poor people certainly didn't! Pharaohs and rich people held fantastic feasts, at which they ate juicy pieces of beef, mutton (sheep), or goose. The meat was sometimes barbecued and served with crunchy onions or garlic, as well as spinach, leeks, peas, or beans. What was for dessert? Juicy figs, sweet melons, or pomegranates.

Who looked really cool?

Egypt is a very hot country, and in ancient times people kept cool by wearing as little as possible. Ordinary workers just wore a simple cloth around their waists. But for the rich, the coolest fashion was graceful clothes made from the finest linen.

Linen is made from a plant called flax. It's very hard to prepare, but the Egyptians could spin and weave it into pieces of beautifully light and flimsy cloth.

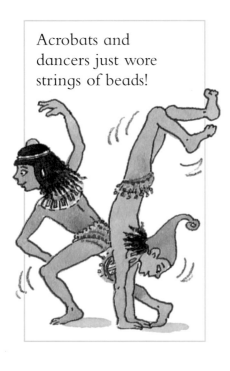

Acrobats and dancers just wore strings of beads!

Women wore long dresses with shoulder straps. Men wore long kilts that hung in folds. Children often wore nothing at all.

Who liked to sparkle?

Most clothes were plain white, so rich people added color and sparkle by wearing beautiful jewelry made from gold and colorful precious stones.

Both men and women wore jewelry.

Sometimes, for a special feast, they wore wide cloth collars decorated with leaves, wildflowers, or glasslike beads. Poorer people's jewelry was made from copper and shells.

Why did shoes wear out?

Servants' shoes were woven from reeds that they gathered from the riverbank. The shoes didn't last long—especially when the servants had to keep running around after their rich masters and mistresses!

21

Who loved wearing makeup?

Rich Egyptian women wore lots of striking makeup. Eyeshadow went on first, then a black line around the eyes, and finally a rosy lipstick and cheek blusher. The ancient Egyptians still look beautiful more than 4,000 years later—in their paintings!

Why did women wear cones on their heads?

Rich women pinned cones to their wigs for feasts and parties. But they wore cones of perfumed grease, not ice-cream cones! As the greasy cones melted in the warm evening air, they gave off a sweet perfume.

The Egyptians loved to smell good. Rich people used scented oils and breath fresheners, and they carried sweet-smelling flowers around with them.

Men also liked to look good, so they wore makeup, too.

The Egyptians took great care of their looks. They mixed up lotions to stop baldness and dandruff— and even pimples!

Who made a beeline for wigs?

Pharaohs and rich people— everybody who was anybody wore a wig on their head. The wigs were made of real hair, which was tied into hundreds of tiny braids and held in place by sticky beeswax.

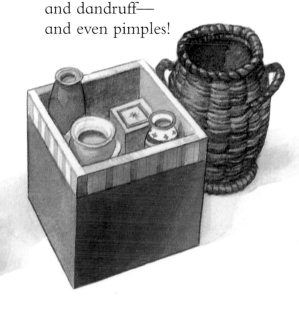

Young boys' heads were shaved except for a single braid of hair on the right-hand side.

Who played with lions?

Children ran around playing ball games or tag and then cooled off with a swim in the river.

Nobody did, if they had any sense! But young children did play with wooden lions and other toy animals. Children also had spinning tops, as well as balls that rattled and dolls with beads in their hair.

Few people could read, so after a day's work they probably sat down to listen to storytellers. There were many exciting tales about gods and goddesses.

Who played board games?

Tutankhamen became pharaoh when he was only 12 years old. He loved playing a board game called senet, and after he died, a board was buried with him in his tomb. It is a beautiful set, made of white ivory and a black wood called ebony.

The senet board had 20 squares on one side and 30 on the other. Experts think that it was a little like the game Parcheesi.

Did Egyptians like parties?

Musicians plucked harps, beat drums and tambourines, blew pipes, and shook tinkling bells.

The Egyptians might have spent a lot of time building tombs, but they weren't a miserable group! They loved music and dancing. At rich people's banquets, there were often shows with dancers, musicians, acrobats, and singers.

Why is paper called paper?

Our word *paper* comes from *papyrus*, the name of a tall reed that grows beside the Nile River. The Egyptians discovered how to use the thready insides of papyrus reeds to make a kind of paper. It was thicker than the paper we use today—but just as useful.

Papyrus paper was expensive because it took so long to make. Quick notes were scribbled on pieces of pottery instead.

1. Paper makers cut and peeled the reeds.

3. They hammered them until the sticky plant juices glued them together.

4. Next, they used a smooth stone or a special tool to rub the surface of the papyrus paper smooth.

2. They cut the reed stems into thin slices and then laid them in rows, one on top of the other.

Few children went to school. Some boys trained as scribes—people whose job was to write. They had to learn more than 700 hieroglyphs. Spelling tests must have been a nightmare!

There were even pictures for numbers. It couldn't have been easy to do math problems!

l = 1		𝌑 = 1000	
∩ = 10		ſ = 10,000	
𝌕 = 100		𓅣 = 100,000	

What did Egyptian writing look like?

The first Egyptian writing was made up of rows of pictures, called hieroglyphs. Each picture stood for an object, an idea, or the sound of a word. Many of the hieroglyphs are quite complicated—they must have taken a long time to draw!

The ends of reeds were frayed to make paintbrushes. Ink was made from soot or red earth.

5. Finally, all the pieces of papyrus paper were glued into a long strip and rolled into a scroll.

The hieroglyphs below make up the name CLEOPATRA. Perhaps you can figure out how to write TOP CAT or LATER.

C L E O P A T R A

Which were the most dangerous animals?

Even hippo hunting could be dangerous. An angry hippo could easily overturn one of the hunters' tiny boats.

Egypt wasn't always a safe place. Wild bulls and lions lived in the desert, while hungry crocodiles lurked in the Nile River. Many Egyptians enjoyed hunting these animals even though they could be dangerous.

When it died, a pet dog was buried with its collar—all ready for a walk in the afterlife!

Did people have pets?

Rich Egyptians had pets, just as we do today, and they loved them just as much. Most people settled for a dog or cat, but people who really wanted to show off kept pet apes and monkeys.

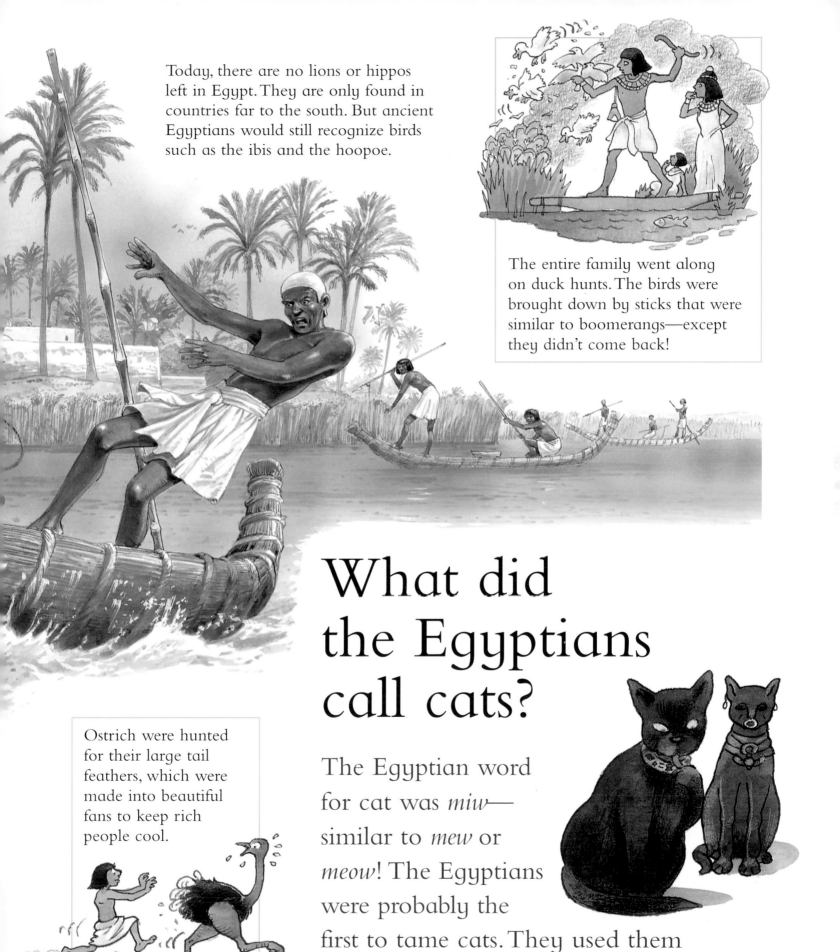

Today, there are no lions or hippos left in Egypt. They are only found in countries far to the south. But ancient Egyptians would still recognize birds such as the ibis and the hoopoe.

The entire family went along on duck hunts. The birds were brought down by sticks that were similar to boomerangs—except they didn't come back!

What did the Egyptians call cats?

Ostrich were hunted for their large tail feathers, which were made into beautiful fans to keep rich people cool.

The Egyptian word for cat was *miw*—similar to *mew* or *meow*! The Egyptians were probably the first to tame cats. They used them to catch mice in grain storehouses.

How can you become an Egyptologist?

Egyptologists are people who study ancient Egypt. To become one, you need to learn all about the history of Egypt and the things that have survived from that time. Reading books and visiting museums are the best ways to start.

Howard Carter went to Egypt in 1892 and spent many years excavating ancient Egyptian tombs. He made his most famous discovery in 1920—the tomb of the boy-pharaoh Tutankhamen.

Tutankhamen's mummy was protected by several coffins. The last one was made of solid gold.

Why do mummies have x-rays?

Modern science is a great help to Egyptologists. X-rays can show whether a mummy died from an illness or an accident. They can even tell whether the person suffered from a toothache!

Egyptologists can even run tests on the things they find in a mummy's stomach and figure out what the person's last meal was before they died!

Where can you come face to face with a pharaoh?

Egypt's largest museum is in the capital city of Cairo. There, you can gaze on the 4,000-year-old faces of the mummified pharaohs. Not all the pharaohs are there, though. Some are still lying peacefully, hidden in their desert tombs.

Index

TITLES IN THE **I WONDER WHY** SERIES

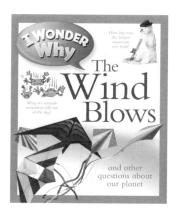